Ina Maka — Mother Earth

Mitákuye Oyásin — We Are All Related

A Lakota phrase that reflects the prayer of oneness and harmony with all forms of life: other people, animals, birds, insects, trees, plants, stones, rivers, oceans, mountains, and valleys

I dedicate this book to all the selfless individuals who have aligned themselves to the one singular feeling that inspires and energizes them to move forward with grace and dignity—LOVE. The love for self, for family and friends, for the environment, and for all of its seen and unseen inhabitants. May you always remember that you are supported and nurtured by the Universe.

And to the children of Mother Earth who understand the value of tolerance, I send you my gratitude and appreciation.

Printed in the United States of America 2024 by IngramSpark. ISBN: 979-8-9876689-0-0

For book queries and more, contact Rachael Blair at kindnessinactionusa@gmail.com.

This is a work of nonfiction supported by research cited in this book. No events have been fabricated.

Decorative illustrations are from commercial licenses obtained from creativemarket.com.

Special recognition and thanks to Stephanee Killen, Book Designer and Owner of Integrative Ink.

Calling all Dream Weavers

Help Endangered Species Survive and Thrive

Written by Rachael Blair

Illustrations by Paul Elegai, Nidi Jangid,
and Master Artist Francis Ekitela

A Note to our Readers
(a must read before you start your dream weaving journey)

In 2009, 4 northern white rhinos arrived at Ol Pejeta Conservancy in Kenya from the Dvur Kralove Zoo in the Czech Republic—2 males (Suni and Sudan) and 2 females (Najin and Fatu). These rhinos were kept safe and in good health. Unfortunately, they were unable to breed despite living in a vast area where they were free to roam. In 2014, Suni died of natural causes, and Sudan (the last northern white rhino male) followed in 2018. I met Najin and Fatu a few months after Sudan had died. I felt very connected to them and wondered what I could do to help. I began working with the United Nations Environmental Program (UNEP), the Rotary Club of Los Altos (California), and the Wildlife Clubs of Kenya to start a project for children in Kenya to expose them to areas of wildlife interest. The project was called "Komba Safaris." Unfortunately, Covid 19 reared its destructive head, and everything shut down. During this time of re-invention, I asked myself how I could manifest something sacred and practical to shift our focus on biodiversity, endangered species, land and ocean protection, water solution management, and soil regeneration. At that point, Paul Elegai, a nineteen-year-old aspiring artist from Laikepia County, Kenya came to my attention, and about two years later, this book came to life.

So, let's begin with a few clarifications to help you take charge of your story.

Specific information on each animal is based on copious research. You will see repeated themes, especially when we talk about threats to each animal. Habitat loss/fragmentation, poaching, and illegal wildlife trade are recurring themes for most animals. It is my intention to represent each animal with the attention and sacredness it deserves; hence, the repetition. I would also urge you to consider that animal population numbers are an estimation in most cases. The International Union for Conservation of Nature is not able to assess accurate numbers every single year. This is why, in some cases, I have included estimates from local conservation organizations and governments who have current data.

The beautiful animal illustrations featured in this book come from three artists who have a deep love and respect for their environment. I thank Paul Elegai, Francis Ekitela, and Nidi Jangid for sharing their gifts with all of us. You are treasured. Of note, Francis is a mentor to Paul and has been for some time now. I would also like to thank my husband, Loudon Blair, for his kiwi illustration and his expertise on the aesthetics of book building. The paintings for the cheetah and African savanna elephant are from his personal photos.

The Conservation Heroines/Heroes need to be recognized, supported, and appreciated for their relentless efforts. As I read their stories, I realized that there are some truly exceptional individuals committed to bringing respect, integrity, and harmony to our planet. The research for each animal took me on a very special journey of discovery and reflection. I am grateful for this opportunity, and I thank all conservation heroines/heroes for hearing the clarion call and living by it.

Spirit Animal Medicine refers to a connection we make with animals and their spiritual wisdom based on our ancestral relationships with them. They can serve as symbols that offer us support and guidance. I thank Ted Andrews for his wonderful book, *Animal Speak — The Spiritual & Magic Powers of Creatures Great & Small*. There is a quote in his book that is deserving of another home.
"If you talk to the animals, they will talk with you, and you will know each other. If you do not talk to them, you will not know them, and what you do not know you will fear. What one fears one destroys." — Chief Dan George (tribal chief of the Tsleil-Waututh Nation, actor, writer, activist from North Vancouver, British Columbia, Canada).

I also give thanks to Lola Pickett for her *Wild Messengers — Alchemical Tarot Guidebook*. The animal messages and affirmations are compassionate and wise. The cosmic animal art by Tanya Casteel is lovely.

Please note that the animal spirit medicine in this book is sometimes in the animal's voice.

Affirmations are positive statements. It is believed that when they are repeated with frequency, you can change the way you think and feel about yourself and others. Your affirmations create a new reality. Every affirmation in this book is a result of my personal experience with each animal (except for the Hirola) and my desire for its wellbeing. I invite you to write your own affirmation about your favorite animal.

The International Union for the Conservation of Nature's Red List of Threatened Species, otherwise known as The IUCN Red List, is the world's most extensive information source on the global extinction risk status of animal, fungus, and plant species. See the definitions below:

Extinct	no reasonable doubt that the last individual has died
Extinct in the Wild	only known to survive in cultivation, captivity
Critically Endangered	species at very high risk of extinction in the wild
Endangered	species at high risk due to **rapid** population decline
Vulnerable	species at high risk due to population decline
Near Threatened	at risk of becoming endangered
Least Concern	species that are abundant
Data Deficient	inadequate information to make an assessment
Not Evaluated	has not been evaluated against the criteria

Currently, there are more than 157,100 species on The IUCN Red List, with more than 44,000 species threatened with extinction, including 41% of amphibians, 37% of sharks and rays, 36% of reef building corals, 34% of conifers, 26% of mammals, 12% of birds, 21% of reptiles, and 28% of selected crustaceans. The IUCN consists of 1,300 governmental and non-governmental organizations and over 14,000 experts. It was created in 1948 to conserve nature.

We thank the IUCN Red List and their partner organizations for their wonderful efforts. All information on this page is from the iucnredlist.org website.

Dream weaving enables us to explore realms of higher consciousness that can help us seek wisdom and guidance. It can help us align to our higher purpose and live a more fulfilling life, which includes the sacred obligation of nurturing and protecting Mother Earth. Before you go to sleep, ask the Universe how you can help endangered species survive and thrive. Write down your dreams, and soon you will start to see a dream weaving pattern. Don't be shy. Tell your family and friends about your dreams and see what all of you can manifest. Work together.

Coral reefs are crucial to ocean health. Please visit the following websites for ocean solutions: Coral Reef Alliance (coral.org), Great Barrier Reef Foundation (barrierreef.org), and Volunteerworld.com (a treasure trove of volunteer opportunities in Australia, Indonesia, Madagascar, Belize, Panama, Mozambique, the USA, the Philippines, and more).

I thank the following artists from Creative Market for their beautiful artwork. You will see decorative art in this book from Top Vectors, Yuliya Derbisheva, PaulaParaula, KitsPix, TheHappyGiftArt, Busy May Studio, Anna Babich, Laras Wonderland, Sans and Sons, Anastezia Luneva, and BarvArt.

All set?

"We are all sacred dreamers, dreaming the world into being."
Alberto Villoldo

Psychologist, Medical Anthropologist, Shaman, Author, and Founder of
The Four Winds Society, School of Energy Medicine and Healing

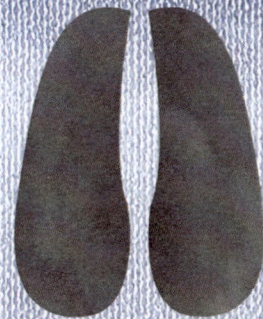

Northern White Rhinoceros

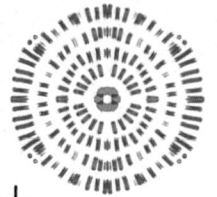

Knowing there are only two remaining, I wanted to paint them, to etch their plight into my mind as I imagined a grieving caretaker, Najin and Fatu, looking away, hoping that somehow their species will survive. – Paul Elegai

Northern White Rhinos in charcoal on watercolor paper

EXTINCT IN THE WILD: There are only 2 northern white rhino left—Najin and her daughter, Fatu. They live under constant armed guard at the Ol Pejeta Conservancy in Laikepia County, KENYA. They are considered to already be extinct by many because these females cannot carry a pregnancy.

There are 5 species of rhino (white, black, javan, sumatran, and greater one-horned). The Sumatran rhino, the Javan rhino, and the black rhino are CRITICALLY ENDANGERED. The greater one-horned rhino is VULNERABLE.

The white rhino consists of 2 sub-species, northern and southern. The southern white rhino is classified as NEAR THREATENED, with over 16,000 remaining (mostly in South Africa).

Rhinoceros comes from ancient Greek and means "nose horn." Rhinos are all grey and eat only plants. They give birth every 2–4 years to one calf at a time, and their gestation period is about 16 months. Rhino horns are made from a protein called keratin (human hair and fingernails are also made from this protein).

Collective noun — a crash of rhinos

Poaching, illegal trade of rhino horns, and habitat loss are their major threats. Over 500,000 rhinos roamed Africa and Asia in the early 1900s. Today, there are approximately 26,000 left in the wild. Their best chance for survival is in national parks and reserves.

HOW are they trying to save this species?

In January of this year, scientists were able to achieve the world's first IVF rhino pregnancy with a southern white rhino. They think they can do the same with viable northern white rhino embryos. The project is called, "BioRescue" and is under the leadership of the Leibniz Institute for Zoo and Wildlife Research in Germany alongside a global consortium of partners from Germany, Italy, Czech Republic, Japan, Kenya, Canada, and the USA.

Ol Pejeta Conservancy needs your help, as they must safeguard a 700-acre enclosure for Najin and Fatu plus provide them with a nutritious diet and intense veterinary care. You can visit and ask for a special viewing. They also have the largest black rhino sanctuary in East Africa.

The International Rhino Foundation has a report you can download from their website detailing the State of the Rhino as of 2023. Poaching continues to be a major threat to all 5 rhino species. They address this multinational issue by protecting rhinos with the assistance of law enforcement agencies, well trained rangers, and community stakeholders. They disrupt wildlife trafficking networks by increasing research and analysis, intelligence gathering, investigations, and wildlife crime prosecutions. They explore ways to reduce and even stop the demand for rhino horns by working with governments to impose stricter penalties for the illegal possession and use of rhino horns.

Northern White Rhino Spirit Medicine — The rhino is tenacious, strong, and passive. It relies on its instincts to survive. The rhino reminds you to embrace your inner strength and power and to trust your instincts. You have the ability to be resilient despite feeling vulnerable. Take charge of your feelings, and do not allow them to overwhelm you. Find time for yourself and know that your environment can heal you.

What you can do to help the Northern White Rhino — BioRescue is working with urgency to develop methods of assisted reproduction and stem cell research to save the last 2 northern white rhino. Go to biorescue.org and click on the donate now page, where you can access "Keep Nature Alive" (crowdfunding for biodiversity). They have videos and information on the amount they have raised so far. Take this to the next level and get your entire school involved, or your employer, by creating awareness. Set up your Round Table of people who want to help and figure out what you can achieve. There is so much power in collaboration, and there are so many people willing and able to help you help them.

Affirmation — NAJIN AND FATU, there are many gifted, compassionate, and honor bound humans who are doing everything in their power to save your species from becoming extinct. I send all these Earth Guardians my love and appreciation. May they have the resilience to work in unity so that one day, I will see you in the wild, with your families, at peace. My dream weaving begins, and you shall remain in my thoughts.

HIROLA

I have never seen a Hirola in the wild, so I was very much inspired by the beautiful markings on its face and horns. It looks very peaceful to me. I hope I get to meet the Hirola one day. I can just imagine how beautiful they look in a group, foraging in their favorite grassland areas. – Paul Elegai

Hirola in charcoal on mixed media paper

CRITICALLY ENDANGERED: According to the IUCN, the loss of the Hirola would be the first mammal extinction on Africa's mainland in modern history. They are the only living member of their genus.

There are 200—500 left in the wild (none in captivity). In the 1970s, there were more than 15,000 hirola antelopes.

They live along the border of Kenya and Somalia. A small, translocated herd can be found in Tsavo East National Park, Kenya. They prefer open grasslands with light bush. They are mostly grazers who feed on short, newly sprouted grass and get most of their water from the food they eat. Their predators are African wild dog, cheetah, lion, and humans.

Their average lifespan is approximately 10 years, and they spend most of their time in small groups of 15—40 individuals. They have unique facial markings (dark glands under their eyes; a white line between and around their eyes; and spiraled, curved horns). Males have thicker horns and dark coats. They are often seen with zebras, gazelles, topi, and oryx.

Collective noun — a herd of hirola

Habitat destruction, competition with livestock, disease, and severe drought are all playing a part in their struggle to survive.

HOW are they trying to save this species?

The Hirola Conservation Program's Founder, Dr. Ali, is doing extraordinary work along with his local team and international partners by seeding areas of land in hirola habitats, fertilization, and bush clearing to give the hirola the best chance to survive and thrive in their protected corridors.

They work with local communities and local government officials who receive training on conservation and implement anti-poaching programs that involve protecting elephants, giraffes, hirola, and other wildlife in the region. They also manage the hirola enterprise, which works with local women and youth groups.

By creating wildlife water access corridors and carrying out vaccination drives for sick wildlife, Dr. Ali and his team maintain biodiversity and infrastructure.

In 2012, with the help of the Northern Rangelands Trust, Kenya Wildlife Services, and the Ishaqbini Community Conservancy (in southeastern Kenya), a predator-proof sanctuary was created to breed hirola, who were then eventually reintroduced into the wild in eastern Kenya. Please see the short film on YouTube about the hirola, Abdullahi Hussein Ali/Kenya/Whitley Awards 2020 (whitleyaward.org), narrated by Sir David Attenborough.

Visit the following website for stories about the Hirola. stories.sandiegozoo.org/zoonooz/hirola-sanctuary/

Hirola Spirit Medicine — Take time to observe your surroundings. Listen. What do you see and hear? Hirolas remind us to use our intelligence and sensitivity to stay safe and be alert. Trust your intuition, that inner voice that speaks to you in a calm and loving manner. Remember, it is wise to surround yourself with others who are kind and who support your hopes and dreams.

What you can do to help the Hirola — Visit Hirolaconservation.org and explore the different ways this non-profit organization in Garissa County, Kenya is addressing the conservation efforts of the hirola antelope. You and your team can help fund habitat restoration, anti-poaching programs, community education, and more. You could also write to them and ask what your school could do to create more awareness about the plight of the hirola. Please note that this is a very remote and volatile area, and it makes conservation efforts very difficult, so they need our attention and support.

Affirmation — HIROLA, may you always have an environment where you can thrive and feel supported by your herd. I appreciate your ability to be aware and to adapt to your surroundings. Thank you for teaching me to be alert as I venture through life. I am grateful for the rangers and caretakers who are working around the clock to save you. I know their work is dangerous at times, so know that I am wrapping you and everyone in white light for protection. I see you thriving in fields of green alongside the gazelles, zebras, and other peace-minded wildlife.

Hawksbill Sea Turtle

I have never seen the ocean, so I am not familiar with marine life.
I wanted to see just how beautiful a sea turtle is by painting it.
– Paul Elegai

Hawksbill Sea Turtle in acrylics on canvas

CRITICALLY ENDANGERED: They are in serious trouble due to constant human intrusion and greed.

They live in tropical oceans, with the largest populations found in Australia, Indonesia, Mexico, the Caribbean Sea, and the Seychelles. They are related to a group of reptiles that lived in our oceans over 100 million years ago and are considered the most beautiful sea turtles because of their colorful shells. Solitary in nature, they travel thousands of miles between nesting and feeding grounds.

They eat sponges, jellyfish, and sea anemones and spend a lot of their time in coral reefs, mangroves, lagoons, rocky areas, ocean islands, and shallow coastal areas. They help our coral reefs by eating the sponges that overgrow on reefs. This sponge overgrowth can cause reefs to suffocate.

They live up to 50 years or more and have very interesting nesting habits. They can lay a minimum of 130 to over 800 eggs in a nesting season. The sex of the turtle is determined by the temperature. Warm nests produce female hatchlings and cooler nests produce male hatchlings.

Collective noun — a flotilla or bale of sea turtles

Loss of nesting and feeding habitats, accidental capture by fishing gear, ocean pollution, illegal wildlife trade, and coastal development are destroying them.

HOW are they trying to save this species?

The World Wildlife Fund works closely with fisheries to eliminate bycatch (when unintended sea turtles and other sea creatures get tangled in gillnets or fishhooks and drown) by helping them switch to turtle-friendly fishing hooks and nets, which are designed to allow larger sea creatures to escape. They track their movement by satellite to keep them out of harm's way and to observe their feeding areas and migration patterns.

Many conservation organizations work with governments to create marine protected areas to secure a safe place to feed, nest, and migrate.

Stopping the demand for the hawksbill tortoise shell—which is used for making jewelry, combs, brushes, and other decorative pieces—involves the cooperation of many tourism companies and conservation organizations that create awareness of this problem. The SEE Shell App can identify whether a product is made from turtle shell or something else. Just download the app and take a picture. There are many resources that can help you avoid turtle shell and report the illegal sale and purchase of it. More information can be found on seeturtles.org.

Plasticoceans.org has an incredible program to end global plastic pollution by informing and mobilizing communities via film activism and collaborating with local communities. "La Voz del Mar: Hope for Hawksbill Turtles" (2022) is another wonderful film, along with many others you can see on wildearthallies.org.

Hawksbill Sea Turtle Spirit Medicine — Wherever you go, please know that home is within you. You are always following your destiny no matter how far you travel. Everything you have experienced has served a purpose. This is how you gain perspective. This is how you remain grounded, determined, and wise. Take your time to do things the right way, and you will see that persistence opens many doors. Think of me as a source of peace when you are feeling scared or even angry and remember that you are part of a creative life force.

What you can do to help the Hawksbill Sea Turtle — Use less plastic. Get your friends and family together and write letters to your local government officials and ask them to do more to remove plastic in our communities. Do not use helium balloons. They can travel long distances and hurt birds and sea creatures. Join the Billion Baby Turtles program that supports more than 20 organizations that protect sea turtles and hatchlings (seeturtles.org). Wildhawaii.org reports that there are fewer than 100 adult female hawksbills in Hawaii. You can help them by donating to their project and keeping the beaches clean and reducing beach lights. For those of us who live in other coastal areas, we can do the same thing. The idea is to keep all kinds of pollution away from our oceans.

Affirmation — HAWKSBILL SEA TURTLE, may you always have pristine waters to live in as you find comfort in clearly seeing all the beautiful sea creatures who, like you, are healthy, abundant, and happy. Thank you for your ancient wisdom and emotional strength.

Rothschild's Giraffe

People on other continents
have never seen the beauty,
grace, elegance, and
majesty of the giraffe.
Being in their presence
reminds me that I have the
ability to walk in beauty
and embrace everything
that makes me unique
and loveable. I think we
sometimes forget just how
special we are.
- Paul Elegai

Rothschild's Giraffe in acrylics

on canvas

CRITICALLY ENDANGERED: While the Rothschild's Giraffe (a sub-species of the Northern giraffe) is considered NEAR THREATENED by the IUCN Red List, some conservationists would argue that the Rothschild's is CRITICALLY ENDANGERED, with less than 3,000 in the wild. The Masai and Reticulated giraffes are both endangered. We have lost over 40% of our giraffe population in the wild over the past 30 years. They are extinct in 7 African countries, and the current estimate for the entire giraffe population is under 100,000.

They live in grasslands, woodlands, or savannahs. They eat leaves, fruit, and stem flowers. They are the tallest living mammal on our planet, and their life span is anywhere between 14—25 years (females tend to live longer). The Rothschild's is the only giraffe with markings that stop halfway down its legs.

Giraffes have very complex social systems and are considered to be very gentle, friendly, and graceful. They are normally seen with wildebeests, zebras, and antelope, and they all play a role in protecting one another. It takes 15 months for a giraffe to give birth, and when the baby is born, it is usually 6 feet tall.

Collective noun — *a tower of giraffes if standing, a journey of giraffes if moving*

Habitat loss due to farming, poaching, hunting, and killing for giraffe meat, civil unrest, and human population growth are destroying our tallest land mammals.

HOW are they trying to save this species?

Initiatives from various organizations include:
Protecting their habitat with local law enforcement agencies (trained and well-equipped ranger forces) and community-based conservation initiatives.

Reducing human wildlife conflict, which includes stopping the demand for giraffe meat.

Implementing de-snaring, anti-poaching, canine units, and response teams.

Stopping the global demand for illegal wildlife products. Poachers have been known to use giraffe bones to make carvings and even trophies.

Providing environmental education to local communities.

Creating rescue centers, orphanages, and rewilding.

During the drought in Kenya from June to November 2022, over 6,000 animals died. Unfortunately, approximately 93 of them were endangered Masai giraffe.

There is hope. Two sub-species of Southern giraffe have thrived due to incredible conservation efforts and now consist of more than 50% of Africa's entire giraffe population.

Rothschild's Giraffe Spirit Medicine — Learn to look beyond the horizon and follow your own path. Follow your dreams, your truth, and your hopes. Don't let anyone bring you down. Be of inspiration to others so that they may find the path that serves their highest good. Remember to be confident and courageous as you move forward.

What you can do to help the Rothschild's Giraffe — Start by visiting savegiraffesnow.org. They have excellent resources on giraffe books, movies, and documentaries. They highlight the new National Geographic movie called "Saving Giraffes: The Long Journey Home." It's about how four conservation organizations (Save Giraffes Now, Northern Rangelands Trust, Kenya Wildlife Service, and the Ruko Conservancy) worked together to rescue 9 endangered Rothschild's Giraffes from a sinking island. It is a lesson on how humans can achieve so much goodwill and hope when they work with wisdom, understanding, and equanimity to solve problems our endangered species face. Wildnatureinstitute.org has a native tree planting initiative, which helps the giraffe, our global climate crisis, and biodiversity. They can create a personal plan for you to become a giraffe hero.

Affirmation — ROTHSCHILD'S GIRAFFE, you walk with such grace and beauty. You appear to be so curious about your surroundings. You remind me that an inquisitive mind creates many opportunities. May you always use your unique perspective to find everything you need to be happy. Thank you for teaching me to have the confidence to ask questions and to pursue my dreams.

African Wild Dog

They are lovely in nature because you don't see them
very often. I am sad they are dwindling. – Paul Elegai

African Wild Dog in acrylics on canvas

ENDANGERED: It is estimated that there are between 4,000 and 6,600 wild dogs left. They have disappeared from 25 out of 39 countries they once called home. The largest populations live in southern Africa and part of east Africa.

They are also called painted wolves and live in savannas, deserts, and woodlands. They can survive in most habitats as long as they have enough space and food to live without threats. They are social animals who work in unison with their pack and look after their sick or old members. They have excellent hearing due to the muscles in their ears that allow them to swivel. They gather in packs of between 10 and 40 and are very loyal to their species and habitat. They can run up to 44 mph and eat more meat than any other carnivore their size.

They hunt medium-sized ruminants like antelopes, giraffes, cattle, and sheep. They are successful hunters due to their ability to communicate frequently, have a life span of about 11 years, and give birth to a litter of 6—20 pups. While lions are their natural predators, humans are considered their biggest threat.

Collective noun — a pack of wild dogs

Habitat loss, disease, illegal snaring—which is a poaching method that is a slow and painful death—and accidental killings are rapidly destroying our wild dogs.

HOW are they trying to save this species?

Endangered Wildlife Trust (ewt.org.za) is having a significant impact on wild dog conservation by implementing the following:

They engage local communities and educate them about the issues they face and introduce solutions to prevent conflict. This is ongoing engagement with the community, as it serves to empower them and see these animals as a vital part of their land and culture.

They have monitoring systems that provide information about wild dog packs in danger (e.g., caught in snares, human wildlife conflict).

They relocate offspring to other reserves to maintain genetic diversity. Habitat fragmentation, such as roads or fences, causes inbreeding, which then results in a loss of genetic diversity. The consequences of this are poor health and the inability to naturally adapt. In fact, adaptation would help them survive environmental changes created by climate change and other man-made conditions.

They provide poison intervention training for rangers and reserve managers.

Worldwildlife.org is creating and safeguarding wildlife reserves and corridors along with governments in eastern and southern Africa to connect critical wildlife habitat, as are other conservation organizations.

African Wild Dog Spirit Medicine — Showing loyalty to a supportive family and community is important. It helps you to become a good judge of character and encourages you to support everyone you care for and respect. When you are part of a team, you benefit from the skills and talents of others, just like they benefit from your skills and talents. It's important to understand the benefits of working well with others and embracing who they are. When you work with a team and take your time to plan and think about the consequences of your actions, you really start to align yourself with the Universe, our teacher and best friend.

What you can do to help the African Wild Dog — Aside from giving to conservation organizations that focus on wild dogs, please consider supporting sustainable tourism. If you are fortunate enough to visit wild dog areas, make sure you use a wildlife tour company that allows you to engage in ethical ways to observe these animals. By supporting their efforts, you are contributing to their rescue. If you want to volunteer, please visit volunteerworld.com to find global opportunities. They work with over 200 organizations in 78 countries and follow the United Nations Sustainable Development Goals.

Affirmation — AFRICAN WILD DOG, I see you roaming over vast lands where there are no fences, no roads, and no humans. Your packs are thriving. You have food and your pups enjoy safe places where they can play and learn from you. You teach them how to communicate for their strength and happiness. You create a life for everyone you love based on loyalty and devotion.

African Savanna Elephant

I started my art journey painting the African Savanna Elephant, so it is my favorite animal to paint.
- Paul Elegai

African Savanna Elephant in acrylics on watercolor paper

ENDANGERED: We have lost about 90% of our African elephants in the last 100 years. There are about 415,000 left across 22 African countries (these IUCN figures include both African savanna and forest elephants). Southern Africa has the highest elephant populations, especially in Botswana. Sadly, the African forest elephant is CRITICALLY ENDANGERED.

The African savanna elephant is the largest mammal on Earth, lives in savannas and grasslands, and can live from 60—90 years. They have large ears and trunks, and both males and females have tusks, which they use for digging holes to find water. Their tusks can weigh over 200 pounds each. They use their trunks for gathering food, water, and communication. They are the only mammal that cannot jump, but they can swim in deep water using their trunk like a snorkel.

They have very complex social structures. The females spend most of their time taking care of their calves. The gestation period is 22 months for a single calf that can weigh up to 200 pounds at birth. They communicate over long distances at low frequencies that can't be heard by humans. They need a large amount of space to eat, drink, and roam and normally spend about 18 hours a day eating.

Collective noun — a herd or a parade of elephants

Poaching for ivory trade, habitat loss due to human encroachment, mining, and logging have decimated their numbers. They have very little wild space left.

HOW are they trying to save this species?

The demand for elephant ivory has created a nightmare for conservationists. Many countries have formed global agreements to ban the international trade of elephant ivory, and the IUCN created a specialist group (AfESG) promoting long-term conservation for elephants.

There are many conservation organizations that are doing incredible work for African elephants like Tusk Trust, African Wildlife Foundation, Wildlife Conservation Society, International Elephant Foundation, Wildlife Conservation Network, Wild Tomorrow, and Save the Elephants. They all have programs that may include anti-poaching initiatives, GPS tracking, monitoring and research, elephant friendly policies, capacity building in elephant range states, and wildlife corridors to give elephants and other animals a safe passage to move and to thrive.

You can join Generation Tusk at tusk.org and be part of a global community of young supporters who are raising funds through various events to promote conservation in Africa.

TRAFFIC.org works to make wildlife trade sustainable, protects our planet's biodiversity, and works to prevent wildlife crime. Perhaps one of the most important things we can do is support their work so that they can stop the demand for ivory, allowing us to focus on creating safe environments for our elephants who are intelligent, self-aware, playful, and compassionate.

African Savanna Elephant Spirit Medicine — It is time for you to sit and listen to your teachers. They can help you understand right from wrong, good from bad, and everything in between. There are times when we just need someone we trust and respect to guide us, to perhaps show us a different perspective. Listen to what rings true to you and create harmony with this awareness. Remember, Earth is a school, and we are here to learn lessons and share our stories with others. Let this wisdom motivate and inspire you.

What you can do to help the African Savanna Elephant — Go to savetheelephants.org and read about The Elephant Queen (2018), an award-winning documentary that changed attitudes in rural Kenya about human-elephant conflict. You can watch it on Apple TV plus and then think about donating funds to support their Human-Elephant Coexistence Toolbox (Advice, Actions, and Tools to Reduce Conflict with Elephants), their elephant scholarships (sponsoring children from pastoralist backgrounds who live in the elephants' range and whose families cannot pay their school fees), and their elephant crisis fund.

Affirmation — AFRICAN SAVANNA ELEPHANT, when I look into your eyes, I feel calm and connected to your wisdom. I trust that you are helping me stay connected to the people and thoughts I cherish and love. I admire how well you take care of one another. I send you affection and protection as you find safe places to roam and watch your calves grow. Thank you for being a kind teacher.

GREVY'S ZEBRA

Here in Ol Jogi, their numbers are rising. This make me happy, so, I felt inspired to create this painting. – Paul Elegai

Grevy's Zebra in acrylics on canvas

ENDANGERED: The IUCN estimates that there are less than 2,000 left in northern Kenya and southern and eastern Ethiopia and 3,000 or less according to the Grevy's Zebra Trust (GZT), an 80% decline since the 1970s. The other 2 species of zebras are the plains zebras (Least Concern) and the mountain zebras (Vulnerable).

Every zebra has a unique striped pattern, just like human fingerprints. You can tell Grevy's apart from other zebras because of their cone shaped, fuzzy ears, brown muzzle, black dorsal stripe, and white belly. They live in dry, semi-desert areas and eat grass, leaves, shrubs, twigs, and bark. They graze 60% of their time and sleep standing up. They are social animals and live in large herds of not just zebras but other animals, such as antelopes and wildebeest. They appear peaceful but can get hostile if they feel scared. One swift kick can kill a grown lion. Their skin is actually black with white stripes.

Grevy's Zebra is named after Jules Grévy, a former President of France in the late 1800s. The emperor of what is now Ethiopia gave him a zebra as a gift.

Collective noun — a dazzle or zeal of zebras

Habitat degradation and loss created by heavy livestock grazing and human encroachment, competition for water, disease, predation, and local hunting for bush meat have created a stressful environment for our Grevy's zebras.

HOW are they trying to save this species?

The GZT is unique, as it is 100% dedicated to saving the Grevy's zebra. They work in partnership with communities in northern Kenya that include the Samburu and Turkana tribes. They employ men and women from the community as Grevy's Zebra Scouts, Ambassadors, and Warriors. The Scouts are mostly women, and their task is to monitor and foster positive attitudes towards the Grevy's zebras. The Warriors do the same thing but must also venture far away from their homes to patrol certain areas. The Grevy's Zebra Ambassadors who are elders, warriors, and women focus on peace initiatives, traditional law enforcement, and grazing management.

They also have a regenerative grazing program to grow healthy plants by breaking up compacted soil to improve rainfall saturation and nutrient absorption. Plants need time to grow and recover after grazing, so they work with communities to figure out an area's recovery time and identify which areas are prohibited from livestock. It's all about planning and bringing people together.

GZT and Ewaso Lions are working together with major infrastructure developers to make certain their railways, vehicle highways, and oil pipelines are re-routed from core breeding areas to safeguard wildlife corridors and to highlight the possible impacts of these infrastructures on biodiversity and pastoralism.

Grevy's Zebra Spirit Medicine — Be true to yourself. This is what makes you dazzle. When you are surrounded by people who nurture, support, and protect the authentic you, you become a beacon and attract opportunities that help you pursue your adventures, dreams, and goals. This is how you stand your ground when you are feeling vulnerable. You call upon your most beloved members of your round table and you listen, ask questions, share your feelings, appreciate the love that surrounds you, and then you TAKE OFF. For you have found your tribe.

What you can do to help the Grevy's Zebra — Go to grevyszebratrust.org and read about all the amazing work that is taking place. The ongoing drought in Kenya between 2020 and 2023 has threatened the lives of so many animals that GZT had to organize feeding operations, outsource hay, and work with national reserve ranger teams to make hay available for the Grevy's zebra and other wildlife. At present, about 10% of their population died of drought-related causes. They also managed water access by constructing dedicated wildlife water points and by digging wells for wildlife use. Send them an email and ask which projects are in most need of financial help and start a school fundraiser. Think of the possibilities.

Affirmation — GREVY'S ZEBRA, thank you for reminding me that I belong to a tribe of not just people but of everything that lives on planet Earth. May I remember to speak my truth, appreciate my free will, channel my strength for good, and protect all living things. I shall dazzle like you.

Cheetah

I am inspired by this cheetah family who live in the Masai Mara.
I would like to see them grow up. – Paul Elegai

Cheetah in acrylics on watercolor paper

VULNERABLE: The latest IUCN report estimates that there are about 6,517 left. Other conservation organizations list the cheetah at approximately 7,100 left in the wild. Most cheetah populations live in Eastern and Southern Africa. Sadly, 90% of cheetahs have disappeared in Africa and 33% live in protected areas. They are almost extinct in Asia with less than 50 left in Iran.

The cheetah is the fastest land mammal (can run up to 70 mph) and the most threatened big cat. They have a very slender body with long legs and a beautiful black line streaming from the bottom of each eye to the corners of their mouth. They live in savannas, grasslands, shrublands, rocky areas, and deserts for up to 12 years in the wild. Their gestation period is 90–95 days, and their litter size averages 2–8 cubs. They hunt during the day and eat medium-sized mammals like warthogs, gazelles, rabbits, and even birds.

Cheetahs are very social. You can see a mother with her cubs or a coalition of males. The female adult cheetah is normally found on her own. A cheetah does not roar. It makes more like a purring, growling, or hissing sound. Luckily, it only needs to drink water every 3–4 days.

Collective noun — a coalition of cheetah

Habitat loss/fragmentation, illegal wildlife trade, conflict with livestock farmers, prey loss due to unsustainable hunting for bush meat, accidental snaring, poorly managed tourism, and road accidents are all threats.

HOW are they trying to save this species?

The Cheetah Conservation Initiative (CCI) works with other conservation organizations that are focused on range expansion, habitat preservation, and safe corridors for cheetahs.

One of their projects consists of rangeland management, which includes grazing planning, protecting conservancies by training community rangers, increasing the capacity of women stakeholders to find alternative livelihoods in the management of the environment, and addressing human-carnivore conflict.

Another huge project is the reduction of illegal bushmeat trade to stop cheetah deaths from wire snares and to improve their natural prey base. Community engagement is crucial to the success of this project. Including more livestock herd protection and using guard dogs makes such a difference in the perceptions of the local community. The Cheetah Conservation Fund's (CCF) Livestock Guarding Dog program claims that farmers with guard dogs are less likely to trap or shoot cheetahs.

The CCF has a livelihood development project that helps communities that live in cheetah areas. They have a gift shop that promotes jewelry and art pieces by local artisans. They help local farmers expand with new initiatives like selling dairy products made from CCF's goat milk, honey products from their apiary, and grapes for wine making.

Cheetah Spirit Medicine — Focus on your vision and do not let distractions stop you from achieving your goals. When you take on too many activities or try to please everyone, you leave little or no time to focus on what motivates and inspires you. Choose wisely and remember that it is very important to take good care of yourself. Being devoted to your health, emotional well-being, education, and sense of adventure is part of the VISION.

What you can do to help the Cheetah — The Cheetah Conservation Fund (cheetah.org) is doing incredible work to save cheetahs, and they would love to have you donate in honor, memory, or support of someone, or support their research and education programs. They have a Peer-to-Peer with JustGiving page where they give you ideas on how to create your own fundraising page. Look at the CCF Events page and see if you can participate. Spend some time visiting their resource library and videos page. They have many videos. You can volunteer in Namibia or help their operations in the U.S., Canada, the U.K, Australia, France, Italy, and The Netherlands. You can also purchase their illustrated children's book entitled, *Chewbaaka — My Life at the Cheetah Conservation Fund.*

Affirmation — CHEETAH, thank you for reminding me that it is okay to take time and look at the landscape around me while I figure out what is deserving of my attention. It is such a unique thrill to watch you run with such perfect harmony. I see you bringing excitement to everyone who is helping you survive and thrive. May you continue to have vast areas of land where you can observe quietly under a tree, take care of your cubs, and run with the wind.

African Leopard

There are two attributes that make the leopard such a special animal—
beauty and elusiveness. It is hard to spot, so when you are fortunate
enough to see one, it is thrilling to be in its presence. It is such
a magnificent big cat. - Francis Ekitela

African Leopard in acrylics on canvas

VULNERABLE: They are the most difficult to see of the African Big Five (lion, rhino, elephant, leopard, and buffalo) and are native to over 35 African countries. They live in savannas, grasslands, deserts, mountains, and rainforests.

African leopards are agile, solitary, and nocturnal in nature. They are very strong and can run up to 58 miles per hour. They can even leap up to 20 feet. They are very good at climbing trees and the only known wild cat to drag their "kill" into trees to keep it safe from predators like lions or hyenas. They eat all kinds of meat (small to large mammals, reptiles, birds, cattle, antelope, sheep, rodents, baboons) and can go without water for long periods of time.

Their coat is covered with rosette-shaped markings on the body and solid black spots on the head, legs, and sides. They have excellent vision that allows them to see 7 times better than humans. Males are much larger than females and have an average lifespan of 10—15 years in the wild. Females give birth to 2—3 cubs per litter, and the cubs remain with their mother for about 2 years.

Collective noun — a leap of leopards

Habitat loss and fragmentation, illegal trophy hunting and killing, decline in prey, and human conflict has resulted in the leopard being one of the most persecuted large cats.

HOW are they trying to save this species?

The San Diego Zoo Wildlife Alliance is working on varied approaches to save the African leopard. Population sustainability is very important, so by monitoring and tracking leopard populations, they determine which conservation measures are the most beneficial. This is vital, as there is very little information on leopard populations. The methods they use for tracking include remote cameras, genetic sampling, and GPS collars. This helps them figure out what is causing the leopard-livestock conflict and what they can do to fix it. They work with local pastoralist communities, conservancies in northern Kenya, and other interested partners to see what can be done to help all concerned.

The Wildlife Conservation Society headquartered at the Bronx Zoo in New York City has an extraordinary team of medical professionals who save wildlife and wild places in over 50 countries. Their One World — One Health initiative combines human, domestic animal, and wildlife health to meet the challenges we face with the loss of species and their habitats, climate change, pollution, and wildlife trade. They are the leader in medical and surgical animal care as well as identifying growing disease threats. They are the oldest zoo-based veterinary program in the world and excel in zoological medicine, wildlife pathology, and conservation health efforts. They have long-term, local programs for big cats making sure they are ahead of any disease that could wipe them out.

Please visit oneworldonehealth.wcs.org and science.sandiegozoo.org.

African Leopard Spirit Medicine — Find your inner power, the feeling within that helps you to face your fears. It provides you with a gift of being able to co-create with the Universe. It guides you to find courage and inspiration. Remember to move with purpose and take good care of your body. It is always sending you messages.

What you can do to help the African Leopard — Panthera.org has a social media kit that you can use to educate your family, friends, and school about how we can save our big cats. Visit Worldlandtrust.org and see which program interests you and start a fundraiser at your school. They have the Keepers of the Wild program that employs men and women as rangers; they have the Plant a Tree program that restores sick ecosystems by planting trees in forest habitats; they have the Buy an Acre of Habitat program to give wildlife room to roam; and they have carbon balanced projects to help you measure your carbon footprint and what you can do to reduce it. As a final thought, it would be wise for you to spend some time understanding what this Trust, along with its partners, have managed to achieve in over 34 years of service to all of Earth's inhabitants.

Affirmation — AFRICAN LEOPARD, even though it is difficult to find you, I know you are there, observing, listening and aware that you are connected to your surroundings. May you continue to roam the vast lands you inhabit free of obstacles so that we can appreciate everything that makes you so unique. I look forward to seeing you one day.

Snow  Leopard

I had never painted a snow leopard before. I had not even seen one. It was a whole new experience for me, very interesting and enjoyable. – Nidhi Jangid

Snow Leopard in Staedtler watercolor pencils

VULNERABLE: They live across a vast region of Asia's high, rocky mountains. They are known as the "ghost of the mountains" because they are very elusive. It is believed that 3,920—6,390 snow leopards remain in their vast home range of 12 countries in central Asia (50—60% of snow leopard habitat areas are in China). They live for 10—12 years.

They have blue, green, or grey eyes and beautiful white fur with dark spots and rosettes, which helps them to blend into their surroundings. Their long tails are good for balance on steep mountains and keep them warm while they sleep. They have big chests to help them draw oxygen from the thin air of the high mountains. They are most active at dawn and dusk and eat mostly wild sheep and goats. The females normally give birth to 2 or 3 cubs and raise them on their own. The cubs normally stay with their mother for almost 2 years.

Since snow leopards are so hard to find, it is difficult to study them. They are not known to attack humans, even if disturbed. They are most closely related to tigers and not leopards.

Collective noun — NONE (they are normally solitary creatures)

Poaching, habitat loss, human wildlife conflict, and climate crisis (rising temperatures will have a devastating impact on their mountainous habitat) have put these beautiful creatures at risk.

HOW are they trying to save the species?

Initiatives from various organizations include:
Conducting tracking, research, and vaccination programs for livestock to reduce their mortality, and income-generating projects (snow leopard handicrafts) for families in snow leopard habitats.

Supporting mobile anti-poaching activities with the help of TRAFFIC, the wildlife trade monitoring network. They are not just killed for their fur; their bones and other parts of their body are used for traditional medicine.

Working with local communities and political allies to make known habitats a national Nature Reserve under the protection of the government.

Understanding and maintaining habitat connectivity across their range.

Training national biologists in conservation teachings.

Working with local communities to stop farmers from killing them by installing predator-proof pens for their livestock.

Creating awareness programs for students and communities. One such program involves a traveling classroom for children where they learn the spiritual and cultural significance of the snow leopard in each region.

Snow Leopard Spirit Medicine — Trust your inner instincts and be courageous. It is important for you to find balance in your life, for this is how you see beyond your surroundings. Observation brings stillness, inner strength, and freedom. Remember to balance your responsibilities by giving them the attention they deserve. This is how you manifest a life where you are receptive to teachings, where you are open to beginnings, and where you can access ancient wisdom. Think of me high up in the mountains when you are feeling unsupported and know that we are connected and aligned with the Universe. You are safe.

What you can do to help the Snow Leopard — There are some fabulous organizations that are dedicated solely to the well-being and protection of the snow leopard. Snowleopard.org has great activities for children you can download, they have partnerships so that you can help them spread awareness, you can volunteer with them, sell their products, host an event, and more. Snowleopardconservancy.org has adoption programs. Panthera.org is a great source of snow leopard information, and snowleopardnetwork.org brings together researchers, conservationists, and snow leopard organizations. Watch the French documentary *The Velvet Queen-Snow Leopard*. It is spellbinding and poignant.

Affirmation — SNOW LEOPARD, your body has adapted to your harsh environment, and the result is fascinating. You spend most of your time alone and yet, you are not alone. Your inner-strength and stillness surround you in a beautiful white light that guides you. May you always have the magic of our mountains to protect and nurture you.

KOALA

Rachael took a photo of a sleeping koala at the Taronga Zoo in Sydney, Australia and sent it to me. I have no experience with koalas, so it was very interesting to see such detail in her photo. The news of the wildfires that raged across Australia filled me with such sadness. I am grateful for the opportunity to paint such a beautiful animal that inspires so much love and compassion.
– Francis Ekitela

Koala in watercolors on watercolor paper

VULNERABLE: The IUCN lists the koala as VULNERABLE, but in February 2022, the Australian government listed the combined populations of koalas in New South Wales, Queensland, and the Australian Capital Territory as ENDANGERED.

According to th IUCN, the koala faces malnutrition and ultimate starvation because of the decline in the nutritional quality of Eucalyptus trees (due to increased CO_2 levels). It is estimated that there are less than 64,000 koalas left in the wild. They once numbered in the millions.

Koalas are marsupials and native to Australia. They live in trees and feed exclusively on the leaves of certain Eucalyptus trees. This limited diet makes them sleepy due to low nutritional content and limited calories. They are mainly nocturnal and solitary animals and move around regularly between their favorite food trees. Their babies are called joeys, and they live in their mother's pouch for about 6 months. Their average lifespan is 15—18 years in captivity and less in the wild. The word KOALA is aboriginal for "no drink" or "no water." Koalas get most of their water from eating fresh eucalyptus leaves. They live in one of the driest continents in the world, and there is only one species of koala on Earth.

Collective noun — koala colonies or koala populations

Habitat destruction, domestic dog attacks, bushfires, disease, and road accidents are causing a tragic decline in their population.

HOW are they trying to save the species?

By creating a Human Plan of Management where community members (land holders, farmers, foresters, activists, educators, researchers, builders, and anyone else interested in protecting Koala habitats) work in harmony to solve the many complexities involved in land-use issues. The Australian Koala Foundation (AKF) explains that the Grand Vision is to create the Koala Kamino consisting of over 2,500 km of prime koala habitat from Cairns to Melbourne.

I strongly recommend you visit the AKF to learn more about their many efforts and to see how you can help (savethekoala.org). Their website is a gold mine of information about koalas and what solutions are coming to the forefront with regard to urban development, current legislation, funding koala research, eco-tourism, tree planting, volunteering, and most importantly, the fabulous programs they have to engage young people in activism. Aussie Ark (aussieark.org.au) and Koalas in Care Inc. (koalasincare. org.au) also deserve your attention. Aussie Ark focuses on Australia's threatened wildlife, and Koalas in Care provide 24-hour rescue services for injured, sick, or orphaned koalas.

Please read *Koala Ark* by Michael Stephen King. The wildfires of 2019 and 2020 decimated many koala populations, and his book is about the bravery and humanity he witnessed despite the tragedy of the wildfires. A percentage of his book sales have been earmarked for Aussie Ark and Koalas in Care.

Koala Spirit Medicine — Learn to express appreciation and gratitude to those who support and nurture you. Remember, gratitude creates a beautiful energy that brings light and joy to your world. It raises everyone's vibration. If you are having difficulties, slow down and pay attention to your surroundings. Step into nature and release any thoughts that do not serve your highest good and take time to find joy in the present.

What you can do to help the Koala — Visit the websites listed and get involved in one of their projects. You can adopt a koala, plant trees, start a school fundraiser, join the Koala Army (savethekoala.com), and share your best ideas with your new Australian family. There are many short videos on koalas, and one that I recommend can be found on YouTube—"Koalas 101" from Nat Geo Wild.

Affirmation — KOALA, may you always have a strong tree that provides you with food, safety, and tranquil sleep under the blissful stars and gaze of our Grandmother Moon and during the warmth and gentle zephyrs of our Father Sun. I think it is very important for you to know that when I observe you, I feel such love and compassion. If everyone on this planet could see you in person, we would all be writing "billets-doux" (French, for love letters) to one another. Thank you for teaching me the value of saying "thank you" to others and for expressing gratitude for all the good things in my life.

K I W I

I was recently in New Zealand, and I encountered the kiwi up close at the Willowbank Wildlife Reserve in Christchurch. I was given the opportunity to draw the kiwi for this book and decided to open my artistic door. I enjoyed drawing this flightless bird from recent memory and tried to capture its nocturnal moonlit environment. – Loudon Blair

Kiwi in colored pencils on mixed media paper

VULNERABLE: There are 5 species of kiwi birds. The IUCN Red List has listed 4 of the 5 species as VULNERABLE and one as NEAR THREATENED. There are approximately 47,700 left. Other figures go as high as 68,000 left.

Kiwis belong to a group of flightless birds called ratites (e.g., ostriches, emus, cassowaries). They are endemic to New Zealand. They live in forests, subalpine scrublands, grasslands, and mountain slopes. They eat mostly earth worms, which satisfies their water needs. The kiwi is more like a mammal, with powerful muscular legs and large feet. They have a very good sense of smell and hearing. Their feathers are more like hair, with patterns that help them to camouflage and keep safe from predators. A kiwi can detect underground movement with its beak, which has sensory pits. It lays one egg, and the incubation period is from 74–84 days.

Some facts from Save the Kiwi state that 50% of all kiwi eggs fail to hatch, 90% of chicks that do hatch are dead within six months, 70% of chicks are killed by stoats (related to weasels and otters) or cats, 10% of kiwi chicks make it past six months old, and 5% or less reach adulthood.

Collective noun — a tribe or raft of kiwis

Extensive clearing of forests, fragmented kiwi populations, and introduced predators (domestic dogs) are the kiwi's ongoing threats.

HOW are they trying to save the species?

New Zealand's Department of Conservation has set up 5 kiwi sanctuaries to protect them from predators and to provide opportunities for research and monitoring. Of note is the impressive statistic that 50—60% of kiwi chicks hatched within the sanctuary survive their first 6 months compared to 11% hatched outside of the sanctuary. They have been partnering with Save the Kiwi and have granted over $7 million to kiwi conservation projects. They have a great program called "Operation Nest Egg," where kiwi eggs or chicks are removed from the wild, hatched in captivity, and raised in nurseries/sanctuaries until they are big enough to be released into the wild. This provides a kiwi bird a 65% chance of survival to adulthood.

They also have 15 captive management facilities that are a great source for creating public awareness, research (e.g., genetics, breeding, habitat requirements, monitoring techniques), and actual kiwi encounters for the public. These nocturnal houses are especially designed to keep kiwis comfortable, safe, and to supplement wild populations when needed.

The National Aquarium of New Zealand has a Kiwi Breeding Program and works with Save the Kiwi Trust.

WWF-New Zealand offers a Community Conservation Fund for projects that conserve and restore New Zealand's native species and natural environments.

Kiwi Spirit Medicine — Be kind. Everything you do should be done with your best intentions, using all your skills, talents, and wisdom. Kiwi is all about community, unity, and working together. Express your emotions with genuine honesty. This will bring you a sense of freedom and strength. In Māori culture, the kiwi is considered a treasure. The Māori people are spiritually connected to their natural environment, and the kiwi represents this sacred bond.

What you can do to help the Kiwi — Start by watching a YouTube film entitled "Kiwi — How does the tiny kiwi bird survive when it can't fly," by Real Wild. Savethekiwi.nz has a lovely online shop where you can purchase items like hats, t-shirts, tote bags, hoodies, children's kiwi books, floor puzzles, kiwi prints, and more to create awareness and to help them with their conservation initiatives. They can help you start a fundraiser and may also be able to put you in touch with a local school that is participating in one of the kiwi sanctuaries. It would be great to team up with them. Just think of the exchange of knowledge you would share. Make a request by sending an email to enquiries@savethekiwi.nz.

Affirmation — KIWI, you live in a magical land with majestic mountains, lush green valleys, beautiful beaches, fiords, rainforests, lakes, and volcanoes. I can see why the Māori named New Zealand AOTEAROA, "land of the white cloud." You are so loved by your native human family that they proudly refer to themselves as kiwis. It is in this spirit that I send you white light for protection, green light for renewal and abundance, and pink light for love. What a supportive and loving family you have.

African  Lioness/Lion

They are being wiped out. Lightning indicates danger. I am creating awareness to all who see my painting. – Paul Elegai

African Lioness in acrylics on canvas

VULNERABLE: Lion populations have declined in Africa and India by about 43% in the last 20 years. The IUCN estimates that there are less than 23,000 left in the entire African continent with Tanzania, South Africa, Botswana, and Kenya having the highest populations. There are less than 700 lions in India, and they are all located in and around the Gir National Park in Gujarat. The IUCN lists the Asiatic lion as ENDANGERED.

Lions live in savannas, dry forests, grasslands, and semi-arid deserts in prides of up to 30 lions. Females do most of the hunting together and take care of their cubs while the males spend more time protecting the area and their pride. Females give birth to a litter of 1–4 cubs every 2 years or so. They have very good night vision, so they normally hunt at night or in the early morning. They can live up to 16 years in the wild and can run up to 50mph. They are apex predators and provide an important role in maintaining a balanced ecosystem by hunting large animals like wildebeests, zebras, gazelles, and warthogs. They prefer zebras and wildebeests because they are easier to catch. They are the second largest big cat. The Siberian tiger is slightly larger.

Lions are very social. Their roars can be heard 5 miles away.

Collective noun — a pride of lions

The biggest threat they face at present is the lack of safe spaces. They are also over-hunted, poisoned, and killed for their furs and other body parts.

HOW are they trying to save this species?

There are many inspirational conservation organizations that are embracing holistic approaches to save our lions. Lionguardians.org recruit Maasai and other pastoralist warriors to collaborate on the best ways to solve conflicts between people and wildlife. The lion guardians empower their communities by teaching them how to reinforce their bomas (homes) to make them lion safe, they monitor lions and find lost herders and livestock, they warn herders if lions are near, and they stop lion hunts. They empower communities that live with wildlife so that they can learn to co-exist as one big family.

Ewasolions.org envisions community-led conservation by creating programs like Mama Simba (designed by Samburu women who embrace conservation efforts), Warrior Watch, Lion Kids Camp, Biodiversity and Infrastructure Program (making sure development projects harmonize with wildlife needs), the Jeremy Lucas Education Fund (scholarships for Kenyan secondary school and university students), and the Community Animal Health Initiative "Kura's Pride" (focuses on local dog health, reduced disease transmission to wild carnivores and a healthier balance between the community, the animals, and the environment). They also manage the challenge of invasive species and how best to restore their landscape with indigenous plants. "Conservation to us, and we hope to you, isn't just about wild animals in faraway mystical places—it's about your memories, your culture, the nature around you and in the world, and how you fit into it. It is part of you, and when you put it into your story, it comes alive." – Ewaso Lions

African Lioness Spirit Medicine — You are not alone. Ask your family, community, and the Universe for help when you need it. This is how you become empowered. You are more powerful when you work with others who are supportive and nurturing. When you do what you love, you attract like-minded people. No need to compete when you have pride in who you are. Radiate strength and courage as you look ahead. Shine your light.

What you can do to help the African Lioness/Lion — There is a beautiful Canadian film called *The Wolf and the Lion* (2021). It's a story about a young woman who rescues a wolf pup and a lion cub, taking us on a journey of tolerance, loyalty, adaptation, and love. We are reminded of the desire and even obligation many of us feel to defend animal rights. Sometimes we need to read stories or watch films about the animals who live on our planet to better understand how we can live together, peacefully. Let this movie be the beginning of your journey in animal rights, tolerance, and biodiversity. Also, Rachael Ignotofsky has a beautifully illustrated book called *The Wondrous Workings of Planet Earth — Understanding Our World And Its Ecosystems*. We are more interconnected than you realize. Let the lioness energy guide you as you begin to help.

Affirmation — AFRICAN LIONESS and LION, you are magnificent to watch. Your beautiful golden colors, your powerful muscles and striking presence always leave me in amazement. Thank you for reminding me to embrace my strength and courage with honor. I see you in a large pride looking at the horizon with serenity. This brings me joy. I shall always walk with you in the light as we illuminate the path.

Leafy Sea

Dragon

I recently discovered the existence of sea dragons at the Birch Aquarium — UC San Diego Scripps Institution of Oceanography located in La Jolla, California. What magnificent creatures. I tried different mediums to bring my leafy sea dragon to life but in the end, I realized my journey was one of discovery. I sketched my sea dragon about 9 times and tried 5 different mediums. Having no art training whatsoever, I thought I could perhaps encourage aspiring young artists to remember that art is all about repeated efforts that express your skill or imagination. In my case, my imagination manifested a purple infused leafy sea dragon swimming in deep waters and bringing light into darkness. - Rachael Blair

Sea Dragon in metallic pencils and glitter on textured card stock

LEAST CONCERN: HOORAY!!!!!

I have included the sea dragon in this book of endangered species to remind you that while our sea dragons are safe, we must keep our oceans clean and reduce bycatch by creating more efficient, gentle, and respectful ways to catch fish.

There are 3 species of sea dragons—the weedy, the leafy, and the ruby. Leafy sea dragons are more yellow and brown (unlike my whimsical drawing) and have many stripes and appendages. They live in the tropical coastal waters of Australia along rocky reefs surrounded by lots of seagrass and kelp. They eat plankton, shrimp, and small fish and live anywhere between 2—10 years. They are slow swimmers but luckily, they are able to camouflage themselves rather well. Their mating ritual consists of a dance where the female deposits around 200 eggs on the male's tail. The eggs are then fertilized and incubated for less than 2 months. When they are ready to hatch, the male shakes his tail to help them along. Only about 5% of the eggs survive. Visit seadragonsearch.org.

Collective noun — NONE (they are normally solitary creatures)

Leafy Sea Dragon Medicine — Be like water and work with the ebb and flow of life. It's like a dance where every move creates harmony, balance, and serenity.

Affirmation — Sea Dragons, I see you thriving in oceans that are pristine in the healthy and brilliant rocky reefs of Australia.

Paul Elegai - Aspiring Artist

This photo was taken at the Ol Jogi Conservancy Rhino Boma (Kenya) in 2023. Paul is sitting with a female, baby black rhino named Bella who was 6 months old. She is very friendly, curious, and is much beloved by staff and visitors.

I am Paul Elegai Akuru from Kenya. I was born in Laikepia County. I am from the Turkana tribe (rhino clan). The Turkana are one of the largest nomadic communities in Kenya. In our culture, animals are very important to us, and we rely on our livestock (cattle, goats, sheep, donkeys, and camels) to feed us and for payment of a dowry.

All my life, I have lived with nature as my best friend and guardian. I was fortunate enough to study at the Ol Jogi Primary School and developed a passion for art. You see, I saw firsthand how our beautiful wildlife was being lost due to human activities, and I felt the urge to do whatever I could to create awareness in my community. Through my art, I hope to bring attention to everyone who values nature and is prepared to take action to keep it safe. I am hoping to go to art school and learn Spanish. I have a great desire to explore the world and learn about our beautiful planet.

I value being a productive, compassionate, kind, and inquisitive young man. As an artist, I feel the beautiful connection between myself and nature. This brings me great joy. I hope my story will motivate you to embrace your dreams and to follow them with harmony and love.

Paul can be reached at paulelegai259@gmail.com.

Francis Ekitela

Artist, Teacher, Conservationist

Francis designed and made this young adult, black rhino cement statue in 2018 at Ol Jogi Wildlife Conservancy. His first one.

Francis graduated from the Buru Buru Institute of Fine Arts (Nairobi) in 2020 thanks to a generous sponsor who was struck by his talent while visiting Ol Jogi in 2017. Francis believes that "inspiring, teaching, and nurturing young talent feels like one of my callings, as an artist. Seeing creative children embrace their artistic gifts gives me a big sense of accomplishment. Helping a child today translates into a direct investment in the happiness and productivity of our children."

He is now the resident artist at the Ol Jogi Wildlife Conservancy and art teacher at their school. He arrived in Ol Jogi at the age of 7 because his parents secured employment there. Luckily, he was able to attend school at the Conservancy and discovered his gift.

"It was in Ol Jogi's school that my passion for art started. My teachers noted my talent and motivated me to continue exploring my art. The environment in Ol Jogi really changed my art life. I started developing a passion for animals, the environment, and realized what could be done through paint and colors. Through my art and teachings, I wish to become a strong advocate for wildlife and the protection of our endangered species, especially our rhinos and elephants."

Francis has created murals, statues, and paintings to beautify the school and to awaken the imagination of all children who have the privilege of learning and experiencing the beauty of wildlife at Ol Jogi.

Francis can be reached at francisekitela@gmail.com.

Nidhi Jangid

University Student

Nidhi and her cat, Simba, are kindred spirits. He has a fondness for paneer (soft cheese) and loves to play. I met Nidhi at her home last year while I was visiting India. Her mother shares her culinary artistry by offering Indian cooking classes to tourists. We spent a fabulous evening learning how to make roti, masala chai, vegetable pulao, mint potatoes, and malai pyaz (creamy onions).

Nidhi is pursuing a Bachelor of Fine Arts degree in Jodhpur, Rajasthan, India. She is 19 years old and started to paint at a very young age. She finds the process of creating art very peaceful and enjoys working with different art mediums. She hopes to become a fine arts teacher once she graduates, and she would also like to start a non-governmental organization for street animals. She believes that all animals are deserving of a good home and is always on the lookout for hurt or abandoned animals she can help. Nidhi has a loving and supportive family.

Dr. Loudon Blair

Engineer, Inventor, Amateur Photographer, Traveler

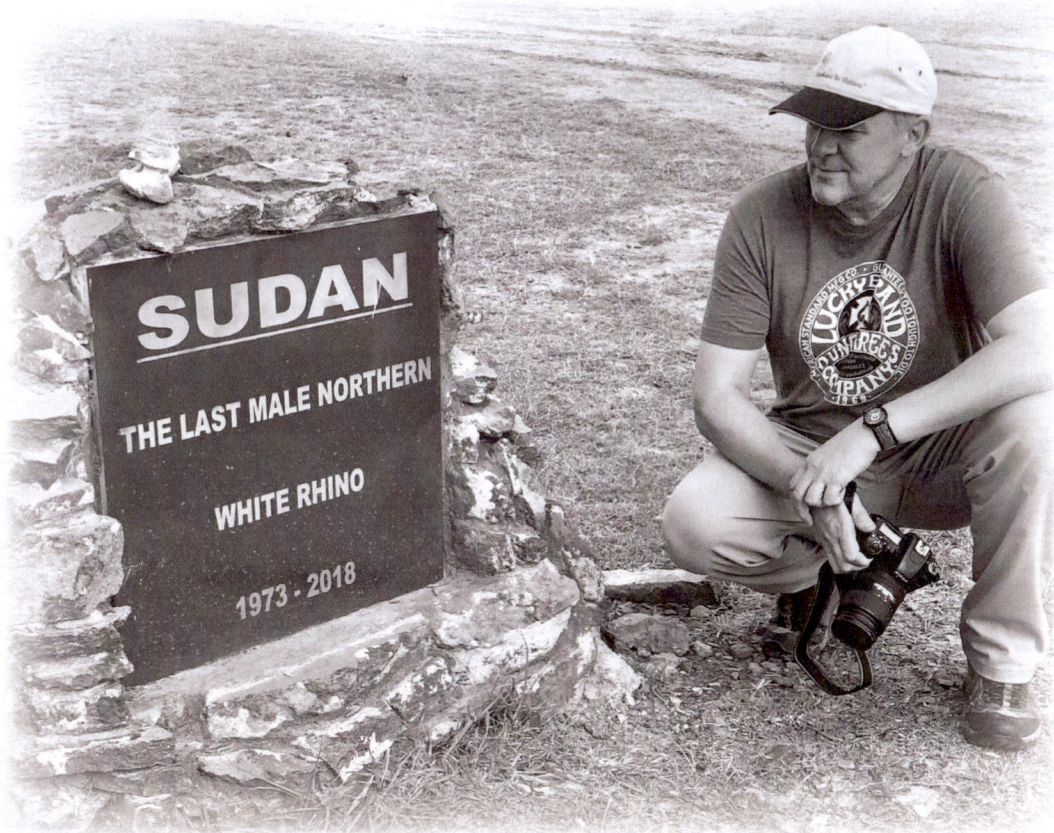

I was born in Scotland and now live in the USA. I remember this moment very well. This photo was taken in 2019 when Rachael and I were working in Kenya for Kindness In Action, USA. I was saddened to see the rhino graveyard at the Ol Pejeta Conservancy and remain hopeful that we can save the Northern White Rhino.

Rachael Blair

Social Anthropologist, Conservationist, Adventurer

I have the good fortune of being able to use my skills, talents, hopes, and dreams to create an environmental program to connect children to wildlife through my non-profit organization, Kindness in Action, Inc. USA. These photos were taken at the Ol Pejeta Conservancy in Kenya in 2018 and 2019, home to Najin and Fatu. I was in awe of their beauty and serenity. It is my hope that with ongoing community awareness campaigns, environmental education for children, an ascension of human values, and a general respect for all inhabitants of Mother Earth, we can reverse the damage we are causing to our biodiversity.

A brief history on how the Universe conspires to make things happen:

Ho'oponopono, Make Our Environment Right, is an environmental project inspired by Najin and Fatu and implemented by Kindness in Action, Inc. USA, with the specific intention of manifesting sacred activism in school children on a global scale. Ho'oponopono is the Hawaiian concept of forgiveness and making things right. The logo was created based on the flora and fauna of the Hawaiian Islands. It is intended to create a sense of well-being and motivation to create a better world—a healthy environment for our children.

Ho'oponopono

Make Our Environment Right

Our **Vision** is to help primary and secondary school children manifest a love for Planet Earth by protecting and caring for her. Our **Mission** is to create a tailor-made environmental curriculum that will create unique environmental initiatives that are in tune with everyone's cultural and spiritual practices. It is our intention that the Hawaiian concept of Ho'oponopono can help students understand how to say they are sorry, how to ask for forgiveness, how to show gratitude, and how to say "I love you" to start the healing process from within to create a catalyst for lasting, positive change.

IMPORTANT CONSERVATION WORDS

Apiary — a place where bees are kept

Apex predator — predators with no natural predators of their own

Biodiversity — many different types of plant and animal life

Bushmeat — wild animals hunted for food

Capacity building — the process of developing and strengthening the skills, instincts, abilities, processes, and resources that organizations and communities need to survive, adapt, and thrive in a fast-changing world

Climate change — describes a change in the average conditions, such as temperature and rainfall, in a region over a long period of time. The National Aeronautics and Space Administration (NASA) scientists have observed Earth's surface is warming, and many of the warmest years on record have happened in the past 20 years

Ecotourism — tourism to areas of ecological interest, especially to support conservation efforts

Elusive — difficult to find, catch, or achieve

Embryo — an unborn or unhatched offspring in the process of development

Gestation period — the condition of being carried in the womb during the period between conception and birth

GPS Tracking — the system of monitoring the location of an object by attaching a global positioning tracking device to it

Habitat fragmentation — when parts of a habitat are destroyed, leaving behind smaller unconnected areas

Human-Wildlife conflict — when encounters between humans and wildlife lead to negative results, such as loss of property, livelihoods, and even life

IVF — in vitro fertilization, a medical procedure whereby an egg is fertilized by sperm in a test tube or elsewhere outside the body

Land use — the purpose for which an area of land is being used (e.g., residential, agricultural, commercial, retail, industrial)

Migration — the movement of an animal from one region, location, or habitat to another in order to breed, grow, or find food

Nutrient absorption in soil — Plants absorb nutrients from the soil through their roots, then move them up through stems in sap

Pastoralist — a sheep or cattle farmer

Poaching — to catch and carry off game or fish illegally

Predation — the preying of one animal on others

Re-wilding — restore an area of land to its natural uncultivated state (used especially with reference to the reintroduction of species of wild animals that have been driven out or exterminated)

Snare — to capture animals by entangling

Sustainable tourism — tourism that takes full account of its current and future economic, social, and environmental impacts, addressing the needs of visitors, the industry, the environment, and host communities

Wildlife Conservancy — A wildlife conservancy is land managed by an individual landowner, a body or corporate, group of owners, or a community for purposes of wildlife conservation and other compatible land uses to better livelihoods.

Wildlife Corridors — an area of habitat allowing for the movement of wildlife populations separated by human activities or structures

Wildlife Reserves — an area of land set aside to protect wildlife species

Sources: Oxford Dictionary, Nasa Climate Kids, UN.org, Verizon, World Wildlife Fund, Woodland Trust, UNEP, Kenya Wildlife Conservancies Association

CONSERVATION HEROINES/HEROES

olpejetaconservancy.org

biorescue.org

africanparks.org

science.sandiegozoo.org

iucnredlist.org

helpingrhinos.org

rhinos.org (International Rhino Foundation)

savetherhino.org

hirolaconservation.org

nrt-kenya.org (Northern Rangelands Trust)

seeturtles.org

plasticoceans.org

wildearthallies.org

wildhawaii.org

worldwildlife.org, wwf.org.au, wwf.org.nz, wwfkenya.org

savegiraffesnow.org

kws.go.ke (Kenya Wildlife Service)

ifaw.org (International Fund for Animal Welfare)

giraffeconservation.org

wildnatureinstitute.org

ewt.org.za (Endangered Wildlife Trust)

tusk.org

elephantconservation.org

savetheelephants.org

wildtomorrow.org

traffic.org

wildnet.org (Wildlife Conservation Network)
awf.org (African Wildlife Foundation)
wcs.org (Wildlife Conservation Society)
grevyszebratrust.org
oneearth.org
conservationmag.org
natgeokids.com (National Geographic Kids)
rewild.org
cheetahconservationinitiative.com
cheetah.org
snowleopard.org
snowleopardconservancy.org
panthera.org
snowleopardnetwork.org
aussieark.org.au
savethekoala.org (the Australian Koala Foundation)
koalasincare.org.au
nationalzoo.si.edu (Smithsonian's National Zoo and Conservation Biology Institute)
oneworldonehealth.wcs.org (The Wildlife Conservation Society)
worldlandtrust.org
lionguardians.org
ewasolions.org
savethekiwi.nz
doc.govt.nz (Department of Conservation, New Zealand Government)
givealittle.co.nz
seadragonsearch.org
oceana.org
aquarium.ucsd.edu (Birch Aquarium at Scripps Institution of Oceanography)

A Tidy Up

Now that you have read this book, familiarize yourself with the United Nations Sustainable Development Goals. There are 17 in total. They will come in handy at school. Go to un.org/sustainabledevelopment/student-resources/ and Worldslargestlesson.globalgoals.org for additional fun resources. Include soil revitalization/rejuvenation in your search. We need soil that is rich and fertile.

Do your research and concentrate on one animal, initially.
Start your project and get as much help as possible. Ask for advice.
Remember your animal spirit medicine and affirmations.
Find books and videos or movies to motivate and challenge you.

More book recommendations:

A Wild Child's Guide to Endangered Animals by Millie Marotta
One World — 24 Hours on Planet Earth by Nicola Davies and Jenni Desmond
Life — A Celebration of Earth's History by Elli Woodard and Dorien Brouwers
Maybe — A story about the potential in all of us by Kobi Yamada and G. Barouch

Use this conservation guide to help you manifest your role as dream weaver extraordinaire for endangered species and purveyor of good health for Mother Earth. The power of good thoughts and wishes is your divine gift.

Thank you for going on this journey with us and remember to DAZZLE. You are our sacred TEACHERS.

"The old Lakota was wise. He knew that man's heart, away from nature, becomes hard. He knew that lack of respect for growing, living things, soon led to lack of respect for humans, too."
Chief Luther Standing Bear

Sicangu and Oglala Lakota Author, Educator, and one of the earliest civil rights heroes in the United States

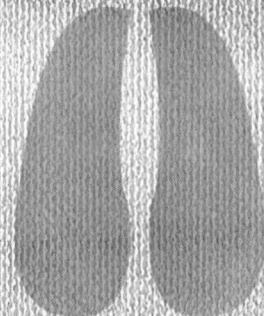

www.ingramcontent.com/pod-product-compliance
Lightning Source LLC
Chambersburg PA
CBRC091537260326
41914CB00022B/1646